It's A Blessing 2 Be A Blessing

DBROCKMAN PUBLISHING PRESENTS:

IT'S A BLESSING 2 BE A BLESSING

A BOOK OF POEMS BY D. BROCKMAN SR.

Prefix

It's A Blessing 2 Be A Blessing

Prefix

It's A Blessing 2 Be A Blessing

IT'S A BLESSING 2 BE A BLESSING

Prefix

It's A Blessing 2 Be A Blessing

Copyrights © *2006 Dexter Brockman Sr*

All rights reserved. Printed in the United States of America. No part of this book may be reproduced and or transmitted in any form or by any means, electronic, mechanical, magnetic, photographic including photocopying, recording or by any information storage and retrieval system without written permission by the publisher or the author. No patient liability is assumed with respect to use the information contained herein. Although ever precaution has been taken in the preparation of this book, the publisher and the author assumed no responsibility for errors or omissions. Neither is any liability assumed for damages resulting from the use of the information contained herein.

ISBN 978-0-9787439-1-8 0

Publisher By:
DBROCKMAN PUBLISHING,
Post Office Box 173208
Tampa, Florida 33672
Local Phone (813) 390-1556
Info@dbrockmansr.info
dbpublisher@yahoo.com

Publishers Note: This is a work of Poetry. The content, incidents, and the dialogue are drawn from the author's thoughts and are not to be constructed as thoughts from others. Any resemblance to actual events or person, living or dead, is entirely coincidental.

Prefix

It's A Blessing 2 Be A Blessing

*For my parents John & Katherine,
and everyone that has the gift of poetry.*

Prefix

It's A Blessing 2 Be A Blessing
Table of Contents

Section	Section	Page
	Introduction	
Intro		iii
April		1
	Situational Poems	
Alone		3
A Toy		4
Manish		5
Persuasive		6
Peaceful Breeze		7
Free Writing		8
Evidence		9
Not A Simple Poem		10
Black in the Days (B.I.D)		11
	Collaboration Poems	
Alone (2001)		13
Greatest Fears		14
A Friendly Conversation		15
Just Cause Pt1-4		17
Special Accounts		22
Ray Day		25
Mrs. (Sweet) Gail		29
	Inspirational	
A Cry		33
Blessed		35
A Childs Prayer		36
Theoretically		37
Greed		39
Just Rambling		41
Liberation		43

It's A Blessing 2 Be A Blessing

The Never Ending Poem	45
Reason For The Season	47
Slanguage	48
To the ones Willing to Receive	50
Ambition	52
Dreams	53
Greatest Fears	55
Faith	56
Differences	58
Conspiracy	59
Evidence	60

Love Poems

Pedestal	62
Too Spesha	63
Open Eye Prayer	65
Another Chance	67
Simple (Love) Poem	68
Written Thoughts of Love	70
Our Lives	72
Captivating Loyalty	73
A Lustful Lie	75

Dedication

Home Going	79
Sheena Tribute	81
Twenty Dollars to Change	83
Mrs. (Sweet) Gail	85
Open Eyed Prayer	88
Mother	90
My Mother	92
Exemplar	94
Emmy Nominees of the Year	96

It's A Blessing 2 Be A Blessing

IT'S A BLESSING 2 BE A BLESSING

It's A Blessing 2 Be A Blessing

dbrockman publishing

It's A Blessing 2 Be A Blessing

INTRO

It's a blessing to be able to become a blessing,
That quote was relayed to me as a lesson,
God handed this gift to me one night while I was resting,
I picked up a pencil a scrap piece of paper then I started testing,
My skills to appeal the attention of others and the knowledge was burning,
My soul. I wrote <u>THE NEVER ENDING POEM</u> to keep my wheels turning.
Looked <u>TO THE ONES THAT'S WILLING 2 RECEIVE</u> when my aunt died 2005,
I watched my family fall to tears but I conquered it with <u>A CRY</u>.
<u>THEORETICALLY</u> we take life for granted & refuse to believe we're <u>BLESSED</u>,
But <u>JUST CAUSE</u> one has a <u>HOME GOING</u> their souls can now rest.
<u>EVIDENCE</u> made me evaluate my life & stop me from living in <u>GREED</u>,
<u>LIBERATION</u>'s soul food, & <u>B.I.D</u> is more than one spoon can feed.

One day I was <u>JUST RAMBLING</u> about the things that's taken place in the last ten years,

It's A Blessing 2 Be A Blessing

My colleague had TWENTY DOLLARS TO CHANGE; in a flash he was faced with his GREATEST FEARS.

From October to APRIL, A CHILDS PRAYER touched souls thru the heart,
John Brockman Sr. my childhood hero, I entitled his poem EXEMPLAR,
I watched a specimen captivate me as I placed her on a PEDESTAL,
I wrote a Simple (Love) Poem, and spit vows thru AN OPENED EYE PRAYER,
Hooked up with some potential poets at work and did RAY DAY,
Shot facts, in NOT A SIMPLE POEM acknowledging nothing gold can stay.
I twisted my tongue went back to my roots as I wrote SLANGUAGE,
I wrote SHEENA'S TRIBUTE then Syniverse started hearing my language.
There's a REASON FOR THE SEASON as THE SPECIAL ACCOUNT BLUES,
The accounts team, in the words of J. Bush the team is "Old News".
This is just a sample what you're about to read, so let your eyes hear,
The last poem is dedicated to 'John & Katherine Brockman' as
THE EMMY NOMINEES OF THE YEAR.

It's A Blessing 2 Be A Blessing
"April"

A- April showers bring May flowers
P- Part of flowers are
R- Roses, roses
I- is a time for
L- Loving and Sharing.

This is my first poem; this poem let me know I had ability to create poetry. I wrote this when I was 10 yrs old. It may not seem like much to you but this started my poetic career.

It's A Blessing 2 Be A Blessing

The Poems that you are about to read, I was inspired to write do to certain situation. I call these.........
<u>SITUATIONAL POEMS</u>

It's A Blessing 2 Be A Blessing
Alone

23sept96

If you're in a field, and feeling all alone,
No one can comfort you, not even at home.
When skies are dark, by the day,
Help is somewhere on the way.
No man has ever failed in the state of success,
They only gave up and let their talents rest.
Life has struggles for children, women, and men,
If one never quit there will never be an end.
For every storm the sun still shine,
This passage has a point and not just a rhyme.
Love is hate, in cases we all hate to love,
We will always fail without the man above.

It's A Blessing 2 Be A Blessing
A Toy

Jan99

There once lived a boy who thought he had a toy.
He decided to dedicate his life to this toy without a joy.
Scenes fell in their presence followers a crowd.
Understandings that were announced drown, and never made
it beyond the clouds.
A for filled room pushed the toy alone with a sigh.
Observe the appearance of time spread, out came a cry.

A shiver from the sun on an aroused and snowy day.
Allowed the boy to exhale and exit outside to play.
Insured he knows the game he play will take a lean.
Above a sunset he sat, enticed how much this toy means.
Intentions were high but at a chance too experienced for risk.
Not knowing the absence of this toy will bring a true mist.
Reuniting of this toy brought a glimmer to his eye.
Apparently the word love has a bond and wont die.

It's A Blessing 2 Be A Blessing
Manish

Defining a man is a concept inverted into the harsh reality, and tampered by trust.

Reliance of a secured failure changes the way we view our temper and constantly ignoring things that is a must.

Deep thoughts that were heart filled, slid through cracks that were abrir but not mentioned till we turn our head.

A soul was once brighten by the abstract that are offered but revealed by the concrete that the body is dead.

It's A Blessing 2 Be A Blessing
Persuasive

My heart's reaching redemption in the up most
way as I cope with my life of phoniness.

My soul is terrified by the obstacle my temple
is suppressing that's forcing me into loneliness.

I hold the far most respect to my heart for
pushing away all negative thoughts that
could have been a visible image.

Who am I per say to judge another exclusive
action when my maturity dismantle all my remedies.

This text was manufacture thru my eyes, my rhythm,
my perception of strength, my soul, thru my words only.

If this Tran of ignorance continue my heart will
incriminate my mind and still I will be Lonely.

It's A Blessing 2 Be A Blessing
Peaceful Breeze

Teardrops spread across the country accumulate enough moist to create a river.
Sweetness is the pale taste our buds feel when the goodness turned bitter.

Wind blowing leaves incriminates the bearing that defectively interrupts the earthly code.
    Peaceful days watching the butterflies are still a concept of the greatest story ever told.

Stormy night is an overlook of how complicated each day is crowding the untamed mind.
    Throughout the darkness temper is released and creates a greedy shine!

Not once did I expect defeat to be a mentor future structure and thoughts.
    Learning to accept failure is a ghost from what we were then, and often taught.

It's A Blessing 2 Be A Blessing
Free Writing

suspiciously influenced by the
manipulation and
the interference that interrupted
this conspiracy
due to the ignorance of evolution
that cause a
significant pollution to our
minority population
which is on the horizon for
respecting the lack of
tolerance from the majority. Informed
one day that
dreams will make this a better society
hypnotizing two birds
flown through the superior atmosphere............
(to be contd)

It's A Blessing 2 Be A Blessing
Evidence

Mirrors spit images that create a reflection
to what we are requesting and
compiles lost thoughts in a familiar direction.
Presenting tangible knowledge everyday we are testing
forcing us to cherish the moment
for each passing second is a chance to turn it all around,
we face reality upside down;
every minute spent looking in the mirror
creates a greater frown.
Tis the season we yell at ourselves
when no one is around,
our ego starts to shrink and our burden
matches us pound for pound.
We watch the moon glow
but never take time to realize
its being assist by a greater star.
We lose track of what's going on here on earth,
to wish we were on Mars.
In actuality the years our world been around
out number the beings that roam it by far.
When we step away from that mirror,
the image captured is placed
within our short term memories,
hoping when we return to it the display
is larger than life,
and falls short of our remedies.

It's A Blessing 2 Be A Blessing
Not a Simple Poem

Can I gather your attention?
for a few seconds so I can mention,
the mysterious ways of our intuition,
how it speaks to us but we don't listen,
we see tight jeans a pair thongs and our eyes start glistening,
pretending we have everlasting intentions,
these thoughts are minimum but we are exposing maximum hypertension,
leading to the water only to deliver retention,
once the plan hit the fan table turn towards redemption,
no one could have warned us but our state of mine was in prevention.

The truth that lies before us, only if we would have had concentration,
of our new revelation, manifested by temptation,
smelling the sweetest perfume granted the demand for immediate relation,
thinking of all the things we will gather from this, including a quick fixation,
not knowing years later she will be apart of your taxation,
when warn the stove is hot listen and disregard the fascination
eighteen year later we wished we would have been in reservation,
four kids three baby mommas later... bruh there will be no relaxation.

It's A Blessing 2 Be A Blessing
Black in The Days

(B.I.D)

Strategically configure remotely queues the depositions in time when we were reminiscing our popular disposition with inconclusive evidence of our American position appointed to men of an alias race with ignorant intentions, took advantage of Lucy's future and place them in suffrage while our men were only counted as three filth of a soul, when they were the ones who put us on their mission, not to mention each obstacle taken reflects back to our ancestors, not only the African culture, but how the color of our skin reflects trouble, they say we are pre-judged to sin. Through whose earthly eyes does this judgment lies for we have been deprived too long to prolong with the old ways trying to re-surface, we'll pack our bags and move to that center they build in space before we let them lace our race, face down in a cotton field or on a plantation bundle up like herd with mild sanitation, sneaking around in the middle of the night just to have relation, and looking beyond the stars for meditation. These are words that were laid upon my heart.
This situation is not real, but it's exactly how I feel.

It's A Blessing 2 Be A Blessing

The Following Poems are Collaborations from people that I knew or worked with. These are the.........
<u>COLLABORATIONS POEMS</u>

It's A Blessing 2 Be A Blessing
Alone (Compilation 2001)

Alone I stand searching this harsh world
for a soul who heart is pure,
Hoping my faith for love will guide me
to someone whose heart is sure.

But yet I stand here, on this harsh brink, in
this uncomforting world crying with the rain,
writing in a tide o' wave of loveless pain.

I still stand awaiting for that pure hearted soul
to swoop down and fear the love-full gain.

Visualizing the beauty of the ocean accepting the
kindness from the clouds, but still before me this
pilgrimage for pureness is so many miles.

A heart so true thine eyes would see a mile beyond
the bluest sea deeper than the darkest trench climbing
over the heavenly fence my soul I'd give to find this
love higher than the stars above.

Is there really a heart so pure a love so high so deep.
As the earth core, now I stand visualizing the beauty
of the ocean feeling the soft touch of the wind roar,
knocking at loves front door.

Stood fast in the silence of the soft wind appreciating
my presence with the mutual concept we share for our
language of love to endure our loneliness…

      Written by: dbrockman, Kawanna Huffman, and
                                          Others.

It's A Blessing 2 Be A Blessing
Greatest Fear

I sit here in my room day after day wondering what the next will bring
Empty thoughts of success as I catch tunes when the birds sing.

Hoping I can succeed in everyway I have planned.
In my heart knowing failure is the greatest fear to man.

The fear I can constantly try to avoid to push aside so I can prosper.
This hasn't just occurred; these fears are from ancient fossils.

Fossils that date way back to our ancestor when they feared man.
Not understanding that our future's already planned.

What about the future we marked for ourselves the path we've walked until now.
How long will this go on, what path shall we choose, what will stop this world from going around.

Written by: dbrockman & Kawanna Huffman

It's A Blessing 2 Be A Blessing
A Friendly Conversation

Disguised by your eyes you walked past my fears...
approaching an experience that's so far, but seem so near...
 the scent of your love made me squirm in disgust..
 I know there something special here, this friendship I will pursue all trust...
gravity tore the fondest of desires...
 we have seen many things, we're about to take this thing for hire....

Your depth grasped my soul it invoked fierce insanity your conversation placed smiles on my heart, making me speak profanity.
Confused, seeking views,
stealing hidden pleasures out of the blues....
finding paths, revoking wraths,
this journey is the after math for me and you...
consoling our sorrows...delighted in better tomorrows...
living day to day not sure of what will stay, I approach this as you're the leader, and I'll follow...
hold my confessions, place them to the test
remembrance forever should I fall from my sacred altar rest...
let go of all memories live for the moment, I want to give you all of me, and don't settle for less....
Spontaneous sincerity is all I have to offer you...
successfully dedicating you my purest definitions
is a gift I've savored prior to your view...

Cont. on next page

It's A Blessing 2 Be A Blessing

this vision has been on trial, and a prediction is without a clue, your persistence to our advancement is nothing new.....

rupturing from captivity the enchantment of my prison you discovered new leaks from my long lost ambition.... I'm in Florida you in Kali, our distance permit a lot will be missing, But we gone tough this out this pilgrimage will be our greatest mission.....

Twin inspirations, clear set directions definite routes, no fear of failure will set the formula for lifelong intentions...

a wise quote was an obstacle that took wrong turns and later pointed toward a clear complexion, we have no worries cause the term 'FEAR' we will never mention.

harsh experiences raped love - prevented many relations......

no fear of rejection cause you are the messiah of my salvations

once that chosen one enter your life your past will be a revelation, and you will not filter your feeling, the experience will be love making and not just temptation...... Written by: dbrockman & Laura

It's A Blessing 2 Be A Blessing
Just cause you are blingin

Just cause you are blingin
Doesn't mean Imma holla
I need more than a fat ride
I need more than spinners
I need more than your Platinum chains
I need a man that is not a boy
I need a man that does not live with his mama
I need a man that can stand up and take care of their offspring
He has to be Tall, strong, Intelligent and treat his woman as a queen
He has to be intelligent enough to stand up to his adversaries w/o having to use violence.
A man like Denzel
A man like Will Smith
Usher is cool
LL is great
Kobe should have stayed in his lane
Just cause you have a big bone
Does not mean that I want a bite
I want a man that can support his family
A man that can be faithful
A man who is fearful of God
A man who is Artistic.
A man that will be mine.   ....Omodele

Cont. on next page

It's A Blessing 2 Be A Blessing
Just cause you are pretty

Just cause you are pretty
Doesn't mean Imma holla
I need more than just a nice face
I need more than a super model
U have to be sophisticated
Elegant like a queen
You must be confident
Dripping with self esteem
And just cause you look amazing
Doesn't mean that you are
I done seen the finest dimes
Get kicked out of a car
I need a phenomenal woman
Like Angela Basset
Like Dianna Carroll
Now those women are classics
Now Beyonce is hot
And Alicia is cool
Eve aint all that
And Lil Kim is a fool
And just cause you sexy
Doesn't mean I wanna bone
I need to make love with your mind
Before I kiss your skin tone
I need to know that you're real
That your life has a purpose
That you're saving for the future
Not wasting money on purses
You see Imma good man
So I can chose to be picky **Cont. on next page**

It's A Blessing 2 Be A Blessing

I can chose between Gina and Pam
And learn secrets from Vicki
So if you are pretty
Just imagine that you are not
Cause if you have a good heart
I'll give you all I got.   .... jamie
bush

                              Just Because
                            You're Fine

Just because you're fine
does not mean that I will give you my time,
You have to earn that from me,
by showing me you are trustworthy,
I'm glad you got all that bling,
but if your soul is black then
your not worth anything,
Can you be in a relationship
and be honest, you know...
tell the truth,
or do I have to be subjected to your lies
and mental abuse?
Can you respect me as I respect you?
Or are you on some I am the man
trip and it is all about you?
Just cause I gave you my number
does not mean I will sleep with you
You can get mad about it if you want
I got some chicken head peeps I could
introduce you to. **Cont. on next page**

It's A Blessing 2 Be A Blessing

They will do what you like and
everything you say,
just cause you gotta a little bling
and they think they are gonna get paid,
but if you are in the market
for a woman that is true,
virtuous and moral,
then I am the one for you.
Understand that a real woman will
look in your eyes and into your soul,
get to know your heart and understand what is
important to you.
So understand that just cause you are fine
does not mean you have the qualities I am looking for
It means that you are good looking and until you prove
otherwise,
that is all it means, nothing more………… **Tammeaka Graham**

Just Be Cause You Can Write

my perception of each of your writings is phenomenal
the emotions and the choice of words are so professional
the energy shared is significantly expressed
some of the thoughts may stir up a mess
we all have different encounters and react to them in our own way
when one is hurt but learn to try again who has the last say
any relationship deserve proper attention gathered on both sides   **Cont. on next page**

It's A Blessing 2 Be A Blessing

discard the things in your past, let your heart be your guide
everyday we set our appearance for someone or something, that's our passion
don't blame the man at the mirror or the girl next to him that's keeping up with fashion
enough fame can bring beauty the human eye process what it continue to see
we should view each commitment as the person is looking thru my eyes staring at me
everyone wants someone that's good for them and a pleasure to the soul
one encounter of an unreleased sighs permits our living as being bold
taking life by the horns living too fast can result the day to be angry
no one would have ever known our talent if it wasn't for the prophecy of Jamie
Tammeaka got skills she touch points making me proud to think out loud
Omodele kept it real and told you how it was, what it is now, so stand proud
these talents were meant to be distributed and brought to our attention
everyone who contribute a poem at work see me at Five O'clock for a poetic detention............... dbrockman

It's A Blessing 2 Be A Blessing
SPECIAL ACCOUNTS BLUES

Once upon a job there was a team that received credentials out of the norm. Late summer the union was created. Strings were pulled, names were drawn, a supervisor was assigned, a meeting took place and then the journey began.

First round pick goes to (BM) <u>Brian Morrison</u> stands out because the job he performs is still unknown among the majority of other team members. At no point anyone would question his abilities or the job he performed.

While (Dan the Man) <u>Daniel Harrod</u> was known as the quiet and innocent one, two weeks of entrapment the goose was loose. The lil egg hatched from the shell.

Then we have <u>Jamie Bush</u> (Ladies Man) a late straggler from the old school, the only person in the entire center that was fired and then rehire four months later. He is also the music man granted to Special accounts to lend a helping hand needless to a part-time ladies man.

Residing next to him <u>Kanhai Rambaran</u> the lo-key (MC flow-master) always keeping his profile professional. Dedication lingers in his cubical, mediation ranges from him to the door. No one truly knows what life has in store for him aside of work. But some of the adventures he tell... I'll leave it at that.

Then there is <u>Roy Edwards</u> (Agent R)... Roy is a boy that had a toy, well was a boy, now he's a man that has gathered a plan to manage anyone that needs a hand in the industry, for writers like you and me, please believe if you need to an agent, that he will be.

It's A Blessing 2 Be A Blessing

Sitting next to me Desmon Jackson (Easy D) contest all his argument by stating "it's a wrap" argument not going his way and desk he would slap, asking you to place it on the wood, and that is that.

The loudspeaker of the group is (Mandy) Amanda Harrison she assures each holiday gets it proper attention. Her ideas are flexible and she has genuine intentions, she's very well spoken and what need to be heard she will mention.

Her counter partner Jasmine Pressley (Soft Spoken) is a true sweetie; her smile opens the joys of any facility out of the norm and stretches miles through her warmth, not to mention the softness release when she speaks. The statement HUH? Would be the next word to speak.

(J-Dog) Justin Emge is wasting his time working for dimes, when he could be equivalent to the Prime......... Minister at some company only if he would step back in line and get his papers as doing himself a favor and gather his degree, then he can be all he can be.

Seretha Aikens (the Gate Keeper) a rude awaken keeps to herself for various reason, but often comes out of her shell to celebrate the season, she's turning her focus closer to a higher being, keeping the faith is the hardest part, her strength will keep her head high and her toes wide to walk with wisdom.

Raymond Roberson (Mr. Patient) he's the one that be the computer wiz, don't know what's stopping him from getting his own biz, his morals pursue patience, never is he in a hurry, but buy far the job always arrive on time.

It's A Blessing 2 Be A Blessing

Then we have our fallen soldiers that departed from us some time ago... Those people shall remain nameless. (Rachael, Chelsey, Michael Mount)... and too our counter partner that has been abducted to our team, they also shall remain nameless (Tyangela, Mike Borden) we welcome you guys. Then we have Tam-Me-Aka. She is our adopted sister that strays in from time to time to keep us in line when needed.

Board Manager Marc Legualt the male of the Executive board, down to earth personality, his relation to the team is phenomenal. We see him as one of us, but only with authority. He's a given, we can retreat to him on any issue, he step aside his character to get it taken care of.

C.E.O Gail Lee she is the backbone of the team, when we need any advise she is there to provide, with listening ears and opened eye, no way would we test her knowledge, she 48 yrs old, there is no doubt that she's wise. Now she is hip to the game don't get it twisted, her favor quote: "everybody in the club getting Tipsy". Her professionalism stains much deeper than that saying. We never take it out of context we understand she just playing.

E.O Shelia Bradley, she is the founder of the group. She believed she could take a group of individuals put them through training, take the knowledge we posse share the knowledge she has. When our backs were against the walls she pushed us to break the wall so we

Cont. on next page

It's A Blessing 2 Be A Blessing

could have a way when they said there was no way. I speak from a team opinion when I say we thank her for that. Then she forms a "Five Hundred Fortune Team." And till this day that's what we are.

As for me, there is more of me to come, go see what I have to show,
Check out my site and see what I'm doing
www.dbrockmansr.info

It's A Blessing 2 Be A Blessing
Ray Day

Back on the old team the hours slipped away
Taking' some "Ray time" shortened the day.
RMG and QA, they paid him no mind,
Sleeping and dozing is how Ray passed his time… Brian Morrison

Man our boy is gone quiet as keep.
Even today we still think he will show up later today as usual.
We will all miss the Deion or Karl Malone pose.
Maybe he will show up and show us the famous picture phone… Desmon

The process is simple, work forty hours and Thurs. was the pay day
All day Friday afternoon the familiar question was "where's Ray"
He made his own schedule and I'm sure on that we all can agree,
Like that time I won the quarter bet when he walked in barely moving his feet…dbrockman

The hacker he was know to be Ray
Hardly at work but that's was his flow Ray
Walked like the man on the moon that had nowhere to go Ray
Drove an old blue fox did not care what nobody think my boy Ray
I believe we will hear around the world someday about a computer wiz our boy Ray… Roy Edwards

It's A Blessing 2 Be A Blessing

There is only so much you can say
About the man who paved the way
To work everyday
As if it was his last day
But damn did he know how to dodge every "Black Friday"
That's why he's our main man Ray… Daniel H

Now we will take a small break for the Cause and a moment in silence for Ray Day

The next two poems are special Tributes

From training class to the fourth floor
Otis was an original spirit for sure
From his designer wrinkled shirts
To the nappiness of his fade
And when it came to omodele's drinks
My dawg always paid
But the homey was a genius
always willing to help
When my computer had a user error
All it took was a small yelp
But it would take him ten minutes
To get to my desk
Cause the boy walked slow
Like fat woman at a food fest

Cont. on next page

It's A Blessing 2 Be A Blessing

But it was the dawg
The latest of them all
My dawg got the tap
And his nameplate is on my wall... Jamie Bush

One of the untouchables when it comes to being Late
and not getting fired
The darkness that posses this individual is yet to be
known "DB dats ur line Dog"
Quiet like a snake in the grass
Over pass by looks
Never gotten written up in the books
Is late move
The wild excuse
Its glad to say he left on his own
Ray
The black late great Sylvester stallone
Over by Jamie desk is where we rest his tombstone.
Please Take
A Moment Of Silent for our Dog
Good Old Ray The Black Sylvester Stallone... Kanhia

It's A Blessing 2 Be A Blessing
Mrs. (Sweet) Gail

She might not be our king
But we are happy to see
That she will continue to be the Queen
Of the Special Account Team......... Dan (The Man) Harrod

They say people come in your life for a season
The thing is you are still here after the reason
Positive words are what she always bless us with
And time for us to bless you with a gift
Your kind words and soft shoulders is always there
Simply because you always care.......... Christopher (Mr. Funny Man) Davis

Ur smile everyday put me in a mood, whether I'm mad, sad or depress
Understanding Sweet and caring is just a few key features that you posses. But I know there's more within Mrs. Gail Where happy that you're still our supervisor
Let god be with us on our Journey on this Earth Because everyday is a turning point in our life
So be happy and cherish every second, minute, hour, days, week's months and years
Because life is filled with highs and lows Happiness and tears Mrs. Gail you will always be our supervisor Even if you was not here.......... Kanhai (MC Low-Key) Rambaran

To be or not to be that was an ever-lasting question,
God placing you in our lives is an eternal blessing.
They tried to replace you to keep you at a distance,

It's A Blessing 2 Be A Blessing

But god is not through with you yet; you now have a new mission.
I'll keep this short and brief as I look through the glass with a smile and say, For those that don't believe, we know you're still here by goodness of God's Grace...
Dex (The Writer) Brockman

When it is all said and done. Gail will always be our supervisor. It will be Gail we will come find to talk to about good and bad news when she or we have left this department. It will be Gail to who we look to for advice and guidance. Gail has looked out for us and protected us from others who thought we to rowdy and didn't work the way they wanted us to. Gail who accepted us and loved us for who we are. Gail is more than a supervisor, she is family. She will always be family...
Rachel (Hotline Hot Girl) Wilcock

Red suit inside Peanut Butter
She is a supervisor like no other
Come to work with a smile every time
Always well dressed like a star, what a dime
Mrs. Gail you're the best supervisor friend
If I was God I would never make these good times
End......... Roy (Agent R) Edwards

The Lord works in mysterious ways and wonders he does perform
And once in a while he will make something special opposite of the norm
And on August 12 1956 he worked his magic again

Cont. on next page

It's A Blessing 2 Be A Blessing

He created a beautiful spirit for the world to befriend
He added some sugar and he added some spice
He added some naughty and he added some nice
But most importantly he added a lot of love
A lot of the kind that comes from the heavens above
Her gave her a touch of class and a heart of gold
He gave her a spirit for the world to behold
If you are lucky enough to meet her you will understand how I feel
The Lord sent us an angel with a heaven sent appeal…
Jamie (The Fly Guy) Bush

It's A Blessing 2 Be A Blessing

These are Poems that I wrote to inspire. I know these poems had to be handed to me as a gift from god. I look back on them and I can still see the situations I was in when I wrote them. Bending Knees.
<u>INSPIRATIONAL POETRY</u>

It's A Blessing 2 Be A Blessing
A Cry

Birth, since Adam and Eve we were meant to conceive to continue our fossils thru multiple generations.

From prenatal an image of two was being created and carried deep within the womb, and to a parent that's a joyful sensation.

Your heart becomes one heart with the figure that's growing inside of you as it continues to mold.

The body have been sculptured and reconfigured to house this first born, as many stories been told.

Not once would you think, for a brief second or a blink that all your care taken days was not sync, and then we search for guidance on what should we do.

"I dressed you in baby blue and you didn't like it, I traded it to pink, late nights of book reading before you were born, even tried to sing, our soul were one, even then my heart was true."

I supplied the necessities, rocked you to sleep the nights you were sick, prayed at your bedside when the devil was in your mist, doing all I can to make your future a brighter day.

From eight weeks to eighteen years old, nine months of pregnancy, seventeen hours of labor, I did what it took at any given time or whatever the price to pay.

How could you turn your back on family do to you've found your significant other, thinking you don't need us you can live your own life.

Cont. on next page

It's A Blessing 2 Be A Blessing

Yea he may have told you you're pretty, and he's really digging you, but baby listen is that enough for you to become his wife.

I can remember watching you play outside, nurturing your wounds, wiping your tears, and even standing and admiring you while you were napping.
I've given you my all still not to satisfy you, stuck my neck out when my love one spoke against you, did all a can to make you happy, this is a cry my child, lay your head in my lap and tell me what happen?

It's A Blessing 2 Be A Blessing
Blessed

You guided me through trials, when my life was at less.
You stayed by my side, when I wasn't as fortunate as the rest.

I once ran out of places to go, you prepared me a nest.
It was you my heart looked upon, the lonely nights I needed to be caressed.

When you were in my presence, I had a lust for the flesh.
Made an attempt to restore the feelings, and reset the fineness.

But the more I tried to recover, I became a bigger pest.
All my future achievements were vanishing, this was stress.

I question my savior why, he replied, "This is a Test."
If your ambition is as strong as your ability, you will always remember, continue to press.

It's A Blessing 2 Be A Blessing
A Childs Prayer

OUR FATHER WHO WATCHES OVER US FROM THE SKIES,
WIPE MY MOTHER TEARS THE LONELY NIGHT SHE CRIES.

MOMMY SAID DADDY LEFT US TO GO SERVE IN HEAVEN AS AN ANGEL
BUT WHEN THINGS GO WRONG SHE ASKS WHY HE LEFT HER WITH THIS ANGER.

DADDY IF YOU'RE UP THERE LISTENING PLEASE ANSWER ME,
IT HURT ME TO SEE MOMMY CRY SO I GET DOWN ON MY KNEE.

I PUSH MY PALMS TOGETHER AND THINK OF THE PRETTY CLOUDS,
I PRAY EVERY NIGHT, MY FAMILY AND I WILL GET TO SEE MOMMY SMILE.

DADDY WE NEED YOU I WISH YOU NEVER HAD TO LEAVE OUR LIFE,
I'M CLOSING MY EYE HARD AS I CAN, I'LL TALK TO AGAIN TOMORROW NIGHT.........
AMEN

It's A Blessing 2 Be A Blessing
Theoretically

Pessimistically Speaking ... The ability to awake one morning enabling myself to only heed from one ear. To many that may be a handicap in which no one would want to hold that designation, personal point of view, that would permit me to only perceive half of the BULL that I in take daily that brings me closer to my qualms.... (Fear)

I often speculate how this world would be if we only had one eye instead of two, this may seem extraordinary, but mental triumphs apprehend our thoughts, critical situations perpetuate our vision, one eye means less tears falling to the earth commencing our greatest suspicions.... (Fear)

Three hundred sixty-five are the quantity of days given, and each moment conceded is a chance to turn it all around, but the immense population can merely envision on Jan 1 each year grants them an opportunity to overcome their worries.... (Fear)

Man's greatest fear is failure. No substance we obtain will ever attain the goals that we set for ourselves to never struggle in this hustle momentum that only strengthen our characters, for which we are actors. Everyday we awake we place ourselves in the frame of mind that we have to dress, walk, speak, and appear to someone out of our normal characteristics to satisfy life's intervention with reality. If we faced the world each day with the personality, perseverance, and ambition that are

Cont. on next page

It's A Blessing 2 Be A Blessing

granted unto us, we fear to be rejected by society. Be you at all times give your all at any cost, never slack from lack of responsibilities being a human wondering this earth is an adventure that can drain one in to misery. Let this world be a stepping stool to be optimistic, and when you have done all your ability allows, don't walk around, just Stand. Let no one manipulate you differently, that Failure is the greatest FEAR to MAN.

It's A Blessing 2 Be A Blessing
'Greed'

I was once inspired to sing love songs,
write love poems,
and lust for a beautiful girl in a thong.
No way could I imagine doing a side by side
with someone whose feelings aren't mutual, so I must hide
behind my pride, until I decide this love things one big joke.
Year after year I've watched my love life collide,
with reasonable gestures I have no one to provide,
these inner emotional overflow,
so I must keep it inside.
My analytical measures have my adrenalin
as If I'm on roller coaster ride,
cosmetic journey influence detour to the heart
that showed no remorse
how two worlds can uniquely unite together for oness,
then burn to flames without a torch,
adventurous moments prohibit everything we worked for
enduring less but wanting more.

We disrespect our hearts by continuing to pollute
our atmosphere with familiar nectars,
we step in new environments
but compare them to similar pleasures,
for we are prone to error,
the significances of our decision making reverse the roles
that we hold but wont let go of what was then,
and its beginning to show.
Restraints keep me from what I feel,

Cont. on next page

It's A Blessing 2 Be A Blessing

*instead of acting on what I see,
that separates me no further from the person that's
taking time to read this acknowledgement that in our
lives we live for GREED.*

It's A Blessing 2 Be A Blessing
"Just Rambling"

Poetry is a potential way to express inner emotions to an out source
I have a lot to say in the next couple lines and I will have no remorse.
Who am I to say right from wrong just gotta get some things off my mind,
this passage was written to have a point and not just plenty of rhymes.

These days we are living consist of pay that don't pertain that we are slaves,
looking into the eyes of our civilization and we can see we are in a raze.
The judicial system has brought comfort to the U.S now we stuck in our ways
and not realizing the problem is within us for we are sleepers walking in a maze.

If you're caught with a suspended license your rights are revoked and you may do time,
a schoolteacher ran over and killed two kids and now its being treated like a petty crime.

Nine eleven was a catastrophe to the United States and I walked away with great anger
but that was no greater than Sodom and Gomorrah when God sent in his own Angels.

The bombing in Oklahoma shook up the entire city early one morning at nine O'clock,

Cont. on next page

It's A Blessing 2 Be A Blessing

McVeigh is sleeping, but still wont bring back the lives
taking at 9:03 when it all stopped.

Hurricane Andrew tow down Homestead in my early
years back in nineteen ninety-two,
history repeats itself in Louisiana the cities are under
water, as a nation what do we do?
The people are in a struggle with nowhere to turn and
survival is there only tool,
instead of helping the culture the system focus on
passing laws, twenty-five years for the ones that loot.

Nothing is new everything that's going on now reflect
our past and has already happened,
I'm just trying to get a point across without pointing
fingers or sound like I'm rapping.

Open your eyes look beneath the clouds for there is more
than we can see,
my aunt died I wrote a poem to life entitled "To the ones
that's willing to receive."

These are hard times; place everything after your faith or
you will come up missing,
one day this entire world would be lifted up to a much
better place, for it was written.

It's A Blessing 2 Be A Blessing
One (Liberation) Conversation

The destruction of life has a familiar hesitation,
opening doors prevail fatal thoughts of revelation,
looking beneath our national curriculum modifying temptation,
appreciating the 400 plus my peoples spent on a plantation,
realizing our great one made no mistakes in our creation,
refusing to defuse the negativity that prohibits meditation,
forty hours a week, fifty-two weeks a year, after the math is formulated it equates to relaxation,
a relapse from ancestor and hidden truth tangles all mean of who and what is placed on probation,
polluting our kids minds, poisons their thought makes them have early relations,
foreseen predictions a mal-positive outcome to replace the upcoming generation,
our thoughts are filled with rubbish compressed so neatly compressed so neatly as if it was emancipation,
trials walk thru walls seeking fears attempting to leave us in tribulation,
we can't let them win, our ambition is greater than their sight what they see is only an abbreviation,
focusing on what right living the respectful path restricts us from heavy precipitation,
believing the 'wills' and dismissing the 'wont(s)' can take tremendous concentration,
when the clouds clear by time, and the sun reset darkness to a normal day, stand proud and give yourself a Standing Ovation.

It's A Blessing 2 Be A Blessing

It's A Blessing 2 Be A Blessing
Never Ending Poem

I sit here today to perform a poem that never end, knowing this mean I would have to lose all sin, state my presences are presently with a friend, and my future reflects on all my kin's, my past often takes me for a spin, thinking of all the things I had to lend, appreciating the rules that I had to bend, one conversation turn boys into men, a lot of these teaching came to me at the age of ten, the goodness throughout my adolescence will always mend, kids these days have more heart than the man made of tin, this world can do a three sixty at the drop of a pin, whites and blacks have a controversy in actuality one is the others twin, I once stepped outside my race and was never excepted back in, criticized from the realization, and acknowledge it with a pen, who are you to state that I can't write a poem that never end....

the never ending poem is a continuation of the greatest story ever told, everything that is presented by life satisfy the pilgrimage that we hold, knotting hills set spiritual standard and interrupt the future mold, reminiscing and contemplating the potential that played apart in parental roles, accepting life and its giving suspends the disturbance of the earth being cold, take time out and think about the opportunities we all sold, no feeling couldn't convert to emotions without significant code, teaching the elders and acknowledging the youth creates a mythical fold, hindering strengths and unreleased sighs permit our living as bold, the discrepancy of our vision is as difficult as an electoral

Cont. on next page

It's A Blessing 2 Be A Blessing

poll, the disappearance of negative aspects is an enhance to my soul, these are the things I want to remember when I get old, tell me what's going to stop this never ending poem from being the greatest story ever told......

It's A Blessing 2 Be A Blessing
"Reason for the Season"

Lawfully lead and spiritually fed,
our lord sent his son as a savior
and upon the cross he bleed.
Ye that is of this world and not saved, is dead.
My soul was cast to dragons,
a question arose, instantaneously I pledge.
Not to use your name in vain as my sanity began to spread.
I stood by the waters and
watched an elder woman as she plead,
to our fearless overseer and then he said:

"Thy sins are forgiven, the faith has saved thee; go in peace"

Chills came over my body, and tears began to shed.
Now I make a joyful noise for the lord,
even if it's just in my head.
I know he's the reason for the season,
but others think its St. Nick instead.
If you don't think so ask yourself each morning,
who allow us get out of bed?
This is not to condone Christmas by far,
so please don't take offense to what's being said.
All I ask of anyone is to keep the Christ in Christmas
or find your identity in a wedge.

It's A Blessing 2 Be A Blessing
"Slanguage"

Dis poem is desined to define dat nollegg is taken from won dat lacs,
And placed wit a few rimes as dey did in back in the times dey all worked on a trac.

Da English dicshonnary was ritten bi a man bac in the day name Webster,
He gane credit for our gramma after the southens scruggled to read in stormi wetha

Webster took alot uv words from diffrent countrys to make da English langwich,
Congradulate to him but der r some peeppa down sout put hem to shame wit a samich.

Day took 26 letta's wich day could harly pre nounce the tru souns,
Day didnt no da diffa from a virb as a akshon word r a nown.

Day made a wae to read in da mist of the nites like hooked on fonics,
Dis lanwich is gettin popula evarady it is now called Ebonics.

In a rcenet sutdy tehy say if a wrod satrt and fnisih whit its lteters the mnid wlil ntoice it,
Helen Keller learned to read is the only equivalence to what they achieved in the mist.

Cont. on next page

It's A Blessing 2 Be A Blessing
I am not triing to nock the gramma dat was put togetha from otha countrys by Webster,
Jus look beneat wats proppa gramma at the cre a shon dose peeppa did and no ders is betta.

It's A Blessing 2 Be A Blessing
'To the Ones Willing To Receive'

I was taught at an early age, I would only receive from you as much as I put into you. Lately I have been doing my duties invest as much as possible into you for one day I will get the full benefit package. The full pension that is allotted to an individual that has place forth the effort and time as I have. Sometime I know I look over my shoulder and venture towards things that may cut my years a little short, or present the opportunity for me to miss out on some minor things that I can really do without. But on the other side I hit all my targets, I make sure that all the bigger and more important things are being handled. I give my savior his time, I witness to those that I feel is in need, try to donate as often as I am able. My savior told me to give till it helps not till it hurts. I know sometime I catch myself judging one for their flaws, and then end up committing a similar sin. With knowledge I know I have the ability recognize my wrong, and correct them with rights. So I just have to ask you life. Each event of my life I participate, does it pay off some type of toll, are my goods weighed according to the wrong that I've done? Can you answer this for me?

Does my action taken affect my family and my other surroundings? If that's the case should I keep a tally of the wrong that I have participated in and divide it by my good standings? I don't generally do things to receive praises from man, so I really wouldn't have a true figure of my good doing. I need answers life. I look upon others who live for fortune, fame, a name, and to be in the eye

Cont. on next page

It's A Blessing 2 Be A Blessing

of man. What is it we are missing life? What is it that we do and not realize it? Could it be the way we awake each morning in concern how well of a day we will have? Could it be how we walk through our place of establishments looking for flaws so we have a reason to find something that's more pleasant to the eye? Could it be the way we look upon our appearance and see it fading so we administer to out source to please the eye of others? Could it be how we have those people in our life that cares for us, but we would rather find someone or something that is pleasant at the time? Life, this letter isn't to pull out my flaws, or knock anyone else. But if, and only if we didn't have that nice apartment/house, if we didn't have that nice car to take us to that nice job that allow us to get nice things. Or if and only if we didn't have those interesting people in our lives, or if we didn't have that big name or that family support to lift us when will we fall, what would we be thankful for? Would we be thankful that we have warm blood running through our vessel, would we be thankful our arteries are disbursing plasma through the body? Or will we be thankful for the simple thought our lungs are pumping a breath of life in our bodies? Life, this letter is not to knock my flaws or the flaws of others; But I would like to apologize for all the things, and all the times that I have taking you for GRANTED.

It's A Blessing 2 Be A Blessing

Ambition

I spent several nights wondering what will happen
if one morning I awoke and the sun didn't rise,
I also wonder how would that affect the moon and the
stars we look upon every night. Those things I can't
control.
They're only mere images compact into thoughts. I once
had the opportunity to turn one of my dreams into
reality.

Truly I can't stop the sun from rising to for fill my
curiosity,
nor can I change the way the Biggest Star has a
tremendous
effect on the moon. If I'm persistent with honesty to my
soul; I know I can accomplish my dreams.
My ambition wont let me quit. And I'll die trying.

It's A Blessing 2 Be A Blessing
Dreams

2july99

The lives we live are arranged by the sequence we follow,
the water we swim in permits a difference by its shallow.
No one has all the answers for every riddle.
How can one judge you, who is the man in the middle?
Don't let life rain get you down always think sunny.
Rehab from the mud and learn to get money.
God sent us upon a pilgrimage with a master and a plan.
When we fall into submerge and peak, we invert into a man.
Ride this bumpy road with an innocent smile.
Float through the stormy nights and hit the clouds.

One minute of every moment equal sixty seconds on a clock.
Mention each moment shared in the now, and "then is a not."
Refer to the inward sustaining the outer visualized as a light.
The closer the view, the dimmer the shine, this vision could me a might.
One encounters a dream by shutting their lids to fantasize.
Upon living out that dream we have to face the world with at least one open eye.
Keep a sharp mind don't let your burdens get you in to steep.
Everything above this line are dreams that make us peeps.

It's A Blessing 2 Be A Blessing

It's A Blessing 2 Be A Blessing
Greatest Fear

I sit here in my room day after day wondering what the next will bring
Empty thoughts of success as I catch tunes when the birds sing.

Hoping I can succeed in everyway I have planned.
In my heart knowing failure is the greatest fear to man.

The fear I can constantly try to avoid to push aside so I can prosper. This haven't just occurred, these fears are from ancient fossil.

Fossils that date way back to our ancestor when they feared
man. Not understanding that our future's already planned.

What about the future we marked for ourselves the path we've
walked until now. How long will this go on, what path shall
we choose what will stop this world from going around.

It's A Blessing 2 Be A Blessing
Faith

3dec97
This world as we know consist of
money, dirt, women, and trees.
There are things kept in a sigh that
our mind and body can't conceive.

It's being tangled in the truth as a
conspicuous night.
Nothings definite, even the fanatical
turns into a might.

Sitting in the faults where the inferior
over views the superior as a whole.
This congested world will be receptacle
to a sheltering cold.

Burning flashes are flowing beneath
our mind at a radical tempo.
Restore the quotes of the great one that
was left as a memo.

Financially stable as we feel the decade
spinning in our hands.
Mentally able as we mature on this
surface without a plan.

No love for one can get you through
the gates like Paul.
But one love in unusual territories that is
what we need for all.

Cont. on next page

It's A Blessing 2 Be A Blessing

No surrender is given without a miniature battle, that's a must.
Believing in God with a passion, that should be your faithful trust.

It's A Blessing 2 Be A Blessing

Differences

June 1999
Temptation and trust walks together hand and hand.
Distinguishing the difference, prophesizes an extension if we can.
One is only lust in the situation at the time.
The other is a myth that separates the nickel from the dime.

Loose fit words spoken in terms of wrath, omits the plan.
Forgiving the blind is the path of an honest man.
Living for one, and only out for you are the tongues of fools.
By releasing these words without context only makes you the pigeon on the stool.

Accepting the fact that we are wrong is in the mind.
Preparing yourself for the worse is like noticing the lemon from the lime.
Permission to perform disrespects the laws of the land.
Experience in this passage enhance the boy and gives everyone the same chance.

It's A Blessing 2 Be A Blessing
Conspiracy

17dec97
Conspiracy is a concept in which
we put power and strength.
Determination is when you put
effort and it is really meant.

Achieving your goal is more than
conquering a good wife.
It pertaining to nothing there no
more uplift in your life.

Carefully observed while your
on the search that's told.
Hindering the myths, disrupting
the futures mold.

Contemporary in an impulsive
remark with no obliterate concerns.
Be careful what you wish for,
life has a natural burn.

Life and death brings an
earthly controversy.
We'll all be on our knees
begging for mercy.

It's A Blessing 2 Be A Blessing
Evidence

Mirrors spit images that create a reflection
to what we are requesting and
compiles lost thoughts in a familiar direction.
Presenting tangible knowledge everyday we are testing
forcing us to cherish the moment
for each passing second is a chance to turn it all around,
we face reality upside down;
every minute spent looking in the mirror
creates a greater frown.
Tis the season we yell at ourselves
when no one is around,
our ego starts to shrink and our burden
matches us pound for pound.
We watch the moon glow
but never take time to realize
its being assist by a greater star.
We lose track of what's going on here on earth,
to wish we were on Mars.
In actuality the years our world been around
out number the beings that roam it by far.
When we step away from that mirror,
the image captured is placed
within our short term memories,
hoping when we return to it the display
is larger than life,
and falls short of our remedies.

It's A Blessing 2 Be A Blessing

I made a vow when I was in High School to not write love poems anymore because anyone could write about love being it was a broad topic. So I stopped writing about love for Years. But when you have a reason to love, love will make away.
<u>LOVE POEMS</u>

It's A Blessing 2 Be A Blessing
Pedestal

Pedestal- a stand, a platform, a podium of some sort
in which something is place upon trusting it can sustain
the weight of the object that will be resting upon it assuring
that it is well capable of supporting the item(s) and gratifying its task.

Beauty- is a physical attraction feasible to the vision,
though its contents aren't concrete for we can see
but cannot touch beauty being it is only a figment in our imagination
and is created through the eye of the beholder.

On this day an article has been placed upon a Podium,
blinded by the intangible of life, ground by the weight of the object,
filled by the image portrayed, and trusted by the potential achievement.
Beauty has been placed upon a pedestal, some see it and believe it,
others touch it and only think it's a figment in their imagination....

It's A Blessing 2 Be A Blessing
Too Spesha

Previous experience embedded my footsteps
and forced me to be unaccepted to your hand.
The paths I chose left breadcrumb traces,
I acknowledge it and alter my plan.

Nights are spent with selfish gestures wishing
one day our roads will meet.
Your perfection of a woman intimidate my
soul and gives my heart a flavoring treat.

I must have lost my marbles, to push away the
greatest feeling known to all man kind.
With all dues paid to respect, thru my vision you're
a Quarter, and I'm degrading myself for a dime.

Confused by my ancient past thoughts, monogamy
drowned
in this decade and love has been hidden within the
clouds. Persistence erect me, reality checked me, our
emotions are in one pod, but we are divided by so many
miles.

The tone of your voice, enhance our conversation,
I receive this as a lesson.
My ears are sensitive to the pureness of your words,
and I honor them as a blessing.

I would never place anything in a passage that
is falsified, everything above this is meant,
This is a cry out from my past, hoping it's not
too late to insert you into my ninety percent.

It's A Blessing 2 Be A Blessing

It's A Blessing 2 Be A Blessing
Open Eyed Prayer

This Poem is dedicated to An Angel (Padget Williams) that took a break From Heaven to spend some earthly time with Dex.

The clarity from her voice gives my heart an everlasting pulse that feeds my brain, as I'm hypnotized.
 I'm astounded each second spent gazing beneath her lashes observing the luxury I gather from the circumference of her pupil that keeps me mesmerized.

 Searching her soul comparing it to any grooves embedded into a ruler for she's fine as the metrics accumulated to create a mile.
 Trying to maneuver through deficits that I'm offered the hand of competition, I'm not trying to be a statistic I want to be around for a while.

 Molesting her emotions keeping them in rhythm prevail every secret of lust for what I was once told.
 Gasping for air trying to grasp the mere thought one day I'll be the one she want to hold.

 Her body is the temple I want to seek walking in the desert fighting against the hottest sand.
 She's my better half, my significant other, without her I feel less than PAR and cheated as a man.

The teaching and the preaching she's overcame from previous struggles she has seen many obstacles that taunted her life.   **Cont. on next page**

It's A Blessing 2 Be A Blessing

This is potential, the one I been seeking, I want to uncover her veil one day and claim her as my wife.

Could she be that absent Angel from heaven stumbling across my path and compressed into the body of an earthly girl?
Excuse my ignorance; the beauty of this wingless creature forfeits any title in equivalent to the word 'WOMAN' she is considered the universe in the capacity of my world.

All my years I've searched for monogamy to respond the things the way they were said, and not what was meant.
Her character builds a future upon facts, that's what separates her from strong women; this is a woman with strength.

I want to glorify this individual, not through an award ceremony, a trophy-issuing banquet, nor receiving the key to the city from the mayor.
I just want my feelings to be acknowledged through these words and an answer to this 'open eyed prayer.'

It's A Blessing 2 Be A Blessing
Another Chance

Her appearance perpetuates my emotions and sends a moist across my lips,
Her womanly fragrances push lust into temptation from the sway in her hips.

Her long curly hair displays beauty and she's more stable than the Red Fern,
The reason she lets go and gives each day another chance I'm willing to learn.

The direction she is going holds my temper as I take it with an adventurous smile,
Her strength gives me a rush, as I blush, getting her is a must; I have patience this could take awhile.

The glossy shine reflects from her lipstick and sends my mind far beyond where I stand,
Don't screw this up Dex, this ones for you, she your second, last, and final chance.

It's A Blessing 2 Be A Blessing
Simple (love) Poem

Love is but the discovery of ourselves that we find in others,
the pleasure is in the delight that we get out of it.
Love is neither concrete nor abstract,
it is an expression shared after a vision becomes reality and the pieces fit.

Many determine love through an act of passion and material things; time is the simplex version of love; one cannot carry over without the other.
Love is a one-syllable word, one definition, one dimension,
two people walking one path, nothing is greater than, equal to, or beneath it not even the love a child has for its mother.

Love is the symbolic features that stare at you every morning while you're at a mirror, and when you least expect it you turn to face a big surprise.
Love is the unfamiliar molecules that our body never recognize, but the heart manage to realize that there is truly a vibe.

Love is fairly simple from where I can see the difficulties arrive when man try to make it be more than it be.
Lesson one and this too apply to you, I, she or he, Love like Jesus loved the churches; I learn that, now I know love starts with in me.

Cont. on next page

It's A Blessing 2 Be A Blessing
*The harder we search for the definition of love
it makes our lives and our days get a little tougher.
But love is the discovery of ourselves,
and that same delight that we can find in others.*

It's A Blessing 2 Be A Blessing
"written thoughts of love"

Listen, take a seat and let me get this off my chest.
Your love is all I have ever needed to get through life's daily test.
I've had several women but you stand out from the rest.
Your beautiful smile, the way you lifted me up when I'm down you are the best.

If God allow me to take one sin to heaven, I would take the sin of lusting for your longing touch.
If I was granted one wish I would trade it to spend the rest of my life with you, for I love you so much.

A flower has to blossom to show the beauty it contains.
On your worst day your beauty is worth a thousand words captured and placed into a frame.

Loving you keep me on my toes, I'm locked in like I'm in a NASCAR Race.
You helped me when I thought I was helpless; I stay high off your love, it's like I've been laced.

You may have the weight of the world on your shoulder; I know things can get hard.
Believe in our love for it is real; remember we were placed together by the will of the Lord.

It's A Blessing 2 Be A Blessing

It's A Blessing 2 Be A Blessing
OUR LIVES

For some time our lives been
tested and our love's been tried
But you've been there for me,
and me for you, we continue to survive

Each morning I think of ways
to give you a daily surprise.
I love you for all the things you've
shown me, like how to compromise

Loving you is like standing in a mirror
looking at me through your eyes.
I compare your life to the book of
Proverbs, for you are so wise.

When I look at you I can see through your
flesh to your soul and I'm hypnotized.
It's like I'm in another world on an Island
staring into the disturbances of an ocean's tide.

Restrains are keeping us away from the
things we want, so I write to improvise.
Keep the faith these trials are a temporary fix,
we will be together for the rest of our lives.

It's A Blessing 2 Be A Blessing
"Captivating Loyalty"

The law of lust permits anyone to not trust
what they think for it may be a raw deal.
> The law of love gives the understanding
> what we have is from above, and its real.

I've searched the entire world to find that perfect girl,
but since Eve ate from the tree we have been living in sin.
> The way we live is not right, an honorable
> woman I want to make you my wife, the faith is
> buried within.

I love you from your cheeks to your toes, I'll love you
more as we grow old, don't let anything damper our plans.
> Tears moisten my pillow each night I rest, you've
> been there for me when I wasn't at my best, it's a
> privilege to say I'm your man.

Being with you is like, someone reset my button of life,
and everything I do with you is like a new experience.
> You've taken the best of me, placed it in your
> world forgave the rest of me, and never hesitated
> when asked for a performance.

They say the eyes are a gateway to the soul, when I look
in your eyes I see the wind blow, a path that consist of
you and I.
> I feed from your positive mentality everyday, the
> love we have will lead the way, don't give up
> continue to try.

It's A Blessing 2 Be A Blessing

Somewhere there is a big whole in the sky, I see your wings but on earth you cannot fly, God has to be missing a perfect stranger.

>Over the years your words has been so kind, lift your head and let your 'Halo' shine, I know you are an earthly angel.

Love is but the discovery of ones self, and that same simple delight that we can find in others.

>Beauty is through the eye of the beholder, you're my soul, my wife to be and not just my child's mother.

At night when you look outside, into those friendly skies, the Stars are talking; listen to what they have to say.

>I'm under those same stars, looking at the faith of our love from a far, though I'm captivated, loyalty will keep our love growing today.

It's A Blessing 2 Be A Blessing
"A Lustful Lie"

A candle lit beneath the finest oil releasing superior fumes was the only light displayed,
The ceiling fan spread the aroma and rotated the flames, which force our image to sway.

My thoughts muted the noises of the world, for I can't believe I was given this chance,
Being face-to-face breathing the same air as you, "I'm about to accomplish whatever you demand."

Temperature began to rise as I de-clothe you while I plastered you with plentiful kisses,
I wouldn't have traded that moment for anything in this world, not even for a million wishes.

Flesh-to-flesh we lay; my fingers began to play, with your nipples to get you moist and aroused,
I lead a stalk of kisses, below your belly button to your mistress; I didn't stop till juices flow while you squealed out loud.

I mounted you chest-to-chest, to give you my all and no less, while my man muscle brushed against your womb,
As you opened wide, between your legs I commenced to glide, the intimacy of intercourse extended through out the room.

I pumped fast up and down, you through it back pound for pound, I'm glad I chose you as the first round pick.

Cont. on next page

It's A Blessing 2 Be A Blessing

You reached up and I felt you moan, it was getting good so I began to groan, I pulverized slow to not make you feel like a trick.

I was a legend in my own world, watching our shadows dance to the music's twirl; shivers acquire from every movement,
A double climax froze the moment in time, the feelings were malicious as if it was a crime, but our love had just been proven.

I rested with you in my arms inhaling the sweets of your unique fragrances, but things were a little strange as I began to open my eye.
I was holding a letter you sent laced with your perfume in my hand, I had a wet spot in my pants, and all of that was driven by...
A Lustful Lie!

It's A Blessing 2 Be A Blessing

The next couple Poems are poems that I dedicated to people that has influenced my life so I decided to Dedicate a Section to them.

1. Home Going – Is a poem I did when my Aunt (Eliza Brockman) passed and I needed something to help me get over the pain. So I decided to write a poem explaining her strength.
2. Sheena Tribute – I wrote when my site manager took another position in the Company. (Syniverse)
3. Twenty Dollars To Change – This poem is Non-Fiction, a colleague (Kanhai Rambaran) came to work one morning and told me he just live that event and asked me to write a poem about it.
4. Mrs. (Sweet) Gail – This poem was written by some employees when our Supervisor was given a release date and one week before her release date the company decided to keep her. (Who has the last Say)
5. Open Eyed Prayer – In 2003 one day I was catching the bus and I came in contact with an Angel (Padget Williams), then All my Prayers began to get answered.
6. Mother – I wrote that poem On Mothers Day to let every woman know one day can not substitute for the things you do everyday.
7. My Mother – This was away to express and give back to my mother (Katherine Brockman) for all the things she has done for me.
8. Exemplar – This was personal, all my writings I

Cont. on next page

It's A Blessing 2 Be A Blessing

9. contribute to women, but I had a strong father (John Brockman Sr.) that played a huge role in my life. This Ones for you Pops.
10. The Emmy Nominees Of The Year – Goes To John and Katherine Brockman, It's truly a blessing to have a supportive mother and a father all their lives, I didn't have that, I had Parents. And til this day that's what they are.

<u>DEDICATION POETRY</u>

It's A Blessing 2 Be A Blessing
HOME GOING
To: Eliza Brockman Feb. 1952 – Feb. 2005

Every breath respire through your body was for a worthy cause, her absence is a gain to heaven, but to earth we see it as a lost.

I know your soul is in a higher place looking upon the family and the love stretch for miles,
there's no need to continue to weep trust that god will handle this, don't be afraid to smile.

It's hard to believe that we are the ones that have to receive these pains; trust me I know it's hard,
believe in what she brought to you, remember, to be absent on earth, is to be present with the lord.

If she could speak to friends and family from heaven she would advise not to cry for me,
for she is resting in a superior environment and her soul has now been set free.

To be a woman maintaining a family is a full time job and to many it's hard to handle,
to ask someone to trade a love one to the heavenly skies is a conflict of a double standard.

Your time was served fighting the deficits you secured your family and stepped up to the plate,
She wouldn't want anyone to sob, for this is a 'Home Going' remember her as more than the LATE.

Cont. on next page

It's A Blessing 2 Be A Blessing

My heart goes out to anyone that were graced the opportunity to get to know the late merchant, this silent prayer stabilize another white robe was placed upon a soul and claimed as Gods Servant.

It's A Blessing 2 Be A Blessing
Sheena Tribute
To: Sheena Strickland

A journey was handed down to an individual
more than three hundred sixty five days ago,
the process performed took precise planning
and some great leaders to open the path.

There were moments the clouds looked darken
the sky took a rotation from its normal trail,
it was you that we all turn to for guidance
without a doubt you captured wrath.

That Friday before 11/24/03 I watch you stand
Next to Tracy A. with your eyes filled in tears,
tears of joy and excitement that you've achieve
what they said wasn't going to happen.

I approached Tracy after the fact congratulated her
on the strength it took to accomplish this task
with the lack of your appearance I only had
a miniature vision, on this ship you're the captain.

Going thru my recollection on the days where
there was unlimited overtime up on 31,
people would pull shifts from 7am til midnight
and supervisors took naps on their lunch in the Hyatt.

You stood strong the period you weren't
able to go home due to procedures had to be in place,
I still think you had a pillow and a blanket under
your desk but was trying to keep it private.

Cont. on next page

It's A Blessing 2 Be A Blessing

Your presence brought shivers to a room that was heated your conversation assured that if it wasn't fix it was next on the agenda, we partied at, Jackson's, turned it out at the Grand Hyatt, prepared for 5/24, feared in Lake Mary, then celebrated one year showing off your bowling arm.

Jan 3rd is the desire due date that has been confirmed by the NSD(New Service Dept) But we as the OSD (Old Serv. Dept) has not did an OSD Create, We will place it into jeopardy, nor will we concur to the fact that you are leaving us Sheena Strickland servant job well done, the departure will hurt but I know when you took this project, you took us all in with open ARMS.

It's A Blessing 2 Be A Blessing
Twenty Dollars To Change
To: Kanhai Rambaran

I'm glad to say I too was once a victim of what I've witness,
This story is incomplete cause the mishap filtered mercy, and dismissed the goodness

Andrew Jackson's presences appeared in a local store of the neighborhood of a young man,
All he wanted was change to start his day but only got controversy when the twenty left his hand.

A large amount of anger was displayed due to the purchase added up to an amount of 30 cent in sum,
The young fellow didn't want any trouble; he just clearly wanted to pay for his innocent pack of gum.

The store clerk burst into an outrage and began to fluster the young fellow with bad language,
The fellow was so astound he instantaneously retaliated throwing the gum hitting the clerk at an angle.

The clerk threatens to call the cops and approached the fellow as if he was loaded with a strap.
The fellow realized he was going to be late for work and this situation is nothing but a trap.

He retreated to his vehicle to part the scenery knowing he wore out his welcome to stay,
As he drove off the stupid clerk tried to copy the numbers from his license plate.

Cont. on next page

It's A Blessing 2 Be A Blessing

Now the story may sound fictional, falsified, to some it may sound crazy, or derange,
But this is a true story one morning a young fellow encountered with twenty dollars trying to get Change.

It's A Blessing 2 Be A Blessing
Mrs. (Sweet) Gail
To: Mrs. Gail Lee

She might not be our king
But we are happy to see
That she will continue to be the Queen
Of the Special Account Team......... Dan (The Man) Harrod

They say people come in your life for a season
The thing is you are still here after the reason
Positive words are what always bless us with
And time for us to bless you with a gift
Your kind words and soft shoulders is always there
Simply because you always care......... Christopher (Mr. Funny Man) Davis

Ur smile everyday put me in a mood, whether I'm mad, sad or depress
Understanding Sweet and caring is just a few key features that you posses But I know there's more within Mrs. Gail Where happy that you're still our supervisor Let god be with us on our Journey on this Earth Because everyday is a turning point in our life
So be happy and cherish every second, minute, hour, days, week's months and years
Because life is filled with highs and lows Happiness and tears Mrs. Gail you will always be our supervisor Even if you was not here......... Kanhai (MC Low-Key) Rambaran

Cont. on next page

It's A Blessing 2 Be A Blessing

To be or not to be that was an ever-lasting question,
God placing you in our lives is an eternal blessing.
They tried to replace you to keep you at a distance,
But God is not through with you yet; you now have a new mission.
I'll keep this short and brief as I look through the glass with a smile and say,
For those that don't believe we know you're still here by goodness, of God's Grace… Dex (The Writer) Brockman

When it is all said and done. Gail will always be our supervisor.
It will be Gail we will come find to talk to about good and bad news when she or we have left this department.
It will be Gail to who we look to for advice and guidance.
Gail has looked out for us and protected us from others who thought we to rowdy and didn't work the way they wanted us to. Gail who accepted us and loved us for who we are. Gail is more than a supervisor, she is family. She will always be family… Rachel (Hotline Hot Girl) Wilcock

Red suit inside Peanut Butter
She is a supervisor like no other
Come to work with a smile every time
Always well dressed like a star, what a dime
Mrs. Gail you're the best supervisor friend
If I was god I would never make these good times
End……… Roy (Mr. Needy) Edwards

Cont. on next page

It's A Blessing 2 Be A Blessing
The Lord works in mysterious ways and wonders he does perform
And once in a while he will make something special opposite of the norm
And on August 12 1956 he worked his magic again
He created a beautiful spirit for the world to befriend
He added some sugar and he added some spice
He added some naughty and he added some nice
But most importantly he added a lot of love
A lot of the kind that comes from the heavens above
He gave her a touch of class and a heart of gold
He gave her a spirit for the world to behold
If you are lucky enough to meet her you will understand how I feel
The Lord sent us an angel with a heaven sent appeal...
Jamie (The Fly Guy) Bush

It's A Blessing 2 Be A Blessing
Open Eyed Prayer
To: Padget Williams

This Poem is Dedicated to An Angel that took a break From Heaven to spend some earthly time with Dex.

The clarity from her voice gives my heart an everlasting pulse that feeds my brain as I'm hypnotized.
 I'm astounded each second spent gazing beneath her lashes observing the luxury I gather from the circumference of her pupil that keeps me mesmerized.

 Searching her soul comparing it to any grooves embedded into a ruler for she's fine as the metrics accumulated to create a mile.
 Trying to maneuver through deficits that I'm offered the hand of competition, I'm not trying to be a statistic I want to be around for a while.

 Molesting her emotions keeping them in rhythm prevail every secret of lust for what I was once told.
 Gasping for air trying to grasp the mere thought one day I'll be the one she want to hold.

 Her body is the temple I want to seek walking in the desert fighting against the hottest sand.
 She's my better half, my significant other, without her I feel less than PAR and cheated as a man.

The teaching and the preaching she's overcame from previous struggles she has seen many obstacles that taunted her life. **Cont. on next page**

It's A Blessing 2 Be A Blessing

This is potential, the one I been seeking, I want to uncover her veil one day and claim her as my wife.

Could she be that absent Angel from heaven stumbling across my path and compressed into the body of an earthly girl?
Excuse my ignorance; the beauty of this wingless creature forfeits any title in equivalent to the word 'WOMAN' she is considered the universe in the capacity of my world.

All my years I've searched for monogamy to respond the things the way they were said, and not what was meant. Her character builds a future upon facts, that's what separates her from strong women; this is a woman with strength.

I want to glorify this individual, not through an award ceremony, a trophy-issuing banquet, nor receiving the key to the city from the mayor.
I just want my feelings to be acknowledged through these words and an answer to this 'open eyed prayer.'

It's A Blessing 2 Be A Blessing
Mothers
To: All women, Mother or Not

When can one try to describe the pride one takes as being a mother?
As if it's winning a prize in a relay and not reacting to visualize the pain Mary felt as she watched her son sit on the cross to die.

Where's the dignity we were taught to respect a woman
that worked through shame to live out her name'
MOTHER' so she could go home and claim her fame
by seeing a smile upon offspring's that keeps her sane
and separates her from the dudes of lame,
whose intention spans no further than one thang.

How often we try to imitate the perception of life,
that an un-birth given woman will be the perfect wife,
for she too is the a mother not yet paid the baring price,
but withhold the woman agenda never to surrender
when times get harsh, and appears to leave marks,
the farther you run it always seen you're back where you start.

Who gave anyone the authority to facilitate this one-day out of the three hundred-sixty plus days?
Men complain about how hard we work, a mother's life compared to ours, they live in a maze.
When a woman transmit in the course of many stages, between work, put up with life, going home to slave, over a hot stove, cleaning a house kids have set to destruct all with no help, I'm still amazed.

Cont. on next page

It's A Blessing 2 Be A Blessing

Women convert from girls, society judge them against the world,
setting expectations for them to keep their jewels as clams cherish their pearl,
confuses the concept forcing them to live in a bubble,
men pursuing them only as being a lover,
for the title women hold should be much greater than others,
for the next three hundred sixty-four...... all women are appreciated as being MOTHERS.

It's A Blessing 2 Be A Blessing
My Mother
To: Katherine Brockman

The definition of my mother proceeds to receive the respect for she is foundation of all,
She is the ones I needed, to produce for me when I needed her when I was about to fall.

My mother... never a day turn from darkness her jobs not complete for she had rotating shifts and multiple sessions,
even after she made it home a tremendous lesson was awaiting to be learned for what the great one has presented to her in a form of a blessing.

My mother... how can I attempt to define term that blinds the worm and keep a true vision where this cold world often burn our hopes and aspirations.
I then sit beneath my mothers wings where there is comfort restored to me through massive thoughts I am secured and grounded for meditation.

My mother... wiser than the wises old man standing near the pulpit spitting knowledge to the younger generation knowing one of their hearts are set for premeditation that limits the creation stored in the upbringing whose missing the heroic father figure,
My mother's roles now much greater than she could ever imagine, look back to the things we didn't have but she made it happen four kids thirty-five year of marriage, "mommz you delivered."

Cont. on next page

It's A Blessing 2 Be A Blessing

My mother... her strength and faith keeps her head above the clouds, though she continues to walk that mile then she lifts her head towards the stars and began to smile,

a symbol from the sky signifies her steps are still in style, and being paved to success from an adventurous past that she let go of and continue to compile.... All things that where never receive from others and then Katherine Brockman, you're the woman and this is your hour!

It's A Blessing 2 Be A Blessing
Exemplar
To: John Brockman Sr.

tears fall from my eyes
as i continue to weep.
fears race through my heart
at night while i am asleep.

my sons are in a world of their own
as they watch the back of their eye lids.
resting over them in prayer
to my savior for they are just a kids.

my upbringing was by a figure
that wasn't afraid to lend a hand.
he taught me there is no can't
and through God all things i can.

winners never quit, quitters never win
were the healthy words in a motto.
pains of not becoming a reciprocal
what i've been taught sets struggles for tomorrow.

guilt passes through my pores
to frighten me and my surrounding.
many nights i awake in a puddle of sweat
with dreams of letdown as if i'm drowning.

have my fate been handed to me but
i turned the other cheek to be set free?
in 1996 & 2006 all my manly visions were
visual and my eyes could clearly see.

Cont. on next page

It's A Blessing 2 Be A Blessing

my eyes could see there was never a need
to fear these times and the days of struggles.
everything i needed had been provided
by the man that lay each night next to my mother.

then, now, and for future days to come
i may open doors with thoughts of sorrow.
but i will always remember my father
as being my inspirational childhood role model.

It's A Blessing 2 Be A Blessing
'The Emmy Nominees of the year'
To: John & Katherine Brockman

Nineteen hundred seventy a man met a woman and their acting career began.
She was 15, he was 19, who would have thought 35+yrs ago what they promised in that courthouse still stands.

The road wasn't easy with minor education, working in fields doing what it took to have family pride.
On top of that they had four kids that wasn't old enough to understand their parents had things to hide.

Poverty wasn't in their household, but it was a couple houses down and it was working its way there fast.
Though the Emmy nominees had minimal education, they had enough smarts to make their family last.

Cotton gins, cornfields, cutting parsley, stacking boxes, picking beans, traveling as migrant workers to make bills meet ends.
Their four kids took life as it was handed to them while their parents lived the life as a pretend.

The days of cold weather while they were on their knees farming for pennies wishing better days would come around for a while.
To go home after a long day to see the joys from their kids was enough motivation to make them do it over each day with a smile.

Cont. on next page

It's A Blessing 2 Be A Blessing

A good actor/actress puts themselves in the character filling each role as if it was their personal life.
That's what Hollywood and Broadway is looking for; but all they had was each other she was proud and he was glad to have a wife.

These nominees had to play the roles of characters that really weren't living in poverty, and keep smiles on their faces.
Though they saw burning crosses, nooses, and even heard vicious racial tales, they taught their kids to love all races.

Putting patches on pants, washing clothe in a washtub, two parents, four kids, and a dog in a one-bedroom apartment.
If there really wasn't a God beyond those clouds above it's because God was on earth looking over people like my parents.

The struggles I'm not glorifying but it helped my parents watch their four kids graduate from high school leading to successful passing.
A college graduate, Military retiree, an Electrician, and a Nurse all came from the Emmy nominees and their acting.

Poetry by: Dexter Brockman Sr.

www.ingramcontent.com/pod-product-compliance
Lightning Source LLC
LaVergne TN
LVHW091601060526
838200LV00036B/949